F Horn

Easy Grea Hymns

Instrumental Solos for the Intermediate Soloist

T0080830

Contents

Curnow MUSIC

Selected by James Curnow

Easy Great Hymns
F/E♭ Horn

Arranged by:
Stephen Bulla
Douglas Court
James Curnow
Paul Curnow
Timothy Johnson

Order number: CMP 0864.03
ISBN 90-431-1944-X
CD number: 19.043-3 CMP

Easy Great Hymns

INTRODUCTION

This collection of hymns includes some of the most famous hymns in the history of the church. It includes tunes that are literally from around the world. The arrangements have been created by some of the foremost writers of instrumental music, who are internationally known for their musical compositions and arrangements. The goal of these arrangements is to allow the instrumentalist the opportunity to give praise and adoration to God through their musical abilities.

There is a separate piano accompaniment book available. This accompaniment book will work with all of the soloist books. When an accompanist is not available, the accompaniment CD (included) can be used for performance. This CD will also allow the soloist to rehearse on their own when an accompanist is not available.

The accompaniment CD contains tuning notes at the beginning to allow the soloist to adjust their intonation to the intonation of the compact disc accompaniment. Each arrangement in this collection includes a sample performance with soloist as well as a track with just the accompaniment.

May you enjoy using this collection and find it useful in extending your musical ministry.

Kindest regards,

James Curnow
President
Curnow Music Press, Inc.

1. COME THOU ALMIGHTY KING

Italian Hymn

Felice de Giardini
Arr. James Curnow (ASCAP)

4

2. WHEN I SURVEY THE WONDROUS CROSS

Hamburg

Lowell Mason
Arr. **Timothy Johnson** (ASCAP)

3. FOR THE BEAUTY OF THE EARTH

Dix

Conrad Kocher
Arr. **Dougals Court** (ASCAP)

CMP 0864.03 F/E♭ Horn

4. IMMORTAL, INVISIBLE

St. Denio

Traditional Welsh Melody
Arr. **Stephen Bulla** (ASCAP)

Track: 6 16

5. WHEN PEACE LIKE A RIVER

It Is Well With My Soul
Ville Du Havre

Philip P. Bliss
Arr. **James Curnow** (ASCAP)

6. COME, YE THANKFUL PEOPLE, COME

St. George's, Windsor

George J. Elvey
Arr. **Paul Curnow** (ASCAP)

Copyright © 2003 by **Curnow Music Press, Inc.**

7. O WORSHIP THE KING
Lyons

Johann Michael Haydn
Arr. **Timothy Johnson** (ASCAP)

Track: 9 19

8. TO GOD BE THE GLORY

William H. Doane
Arr. **Douglas Court** (ASCAP)

9. CROWN HIM!
Diademata

George J. Elvey
Arr. **Paul Curnow** (ASCAP)

10. FAIREST LORD JESUS
Crusader's Hymn

Traditional
Arr. **Stephen Bulla** (ASCAP)

Tranquil and flowing (♩ = 72)

D.S. al CODA

EasyGreat Hymns

Instrumental Solos for the Intermediate Soloist

Contents

CURNOW MUSIC

Selected by James Curnow

1. COME THOU ALMIGHTY KING
Italian Hymn

Felice de Giardini
Arr. **James Curnow** (ASCAP)

Track: 3 13

2. WHEN I SURVEY THE WONDROUS CROSS

Hamburg

Track: 4 14

Lowell Mason
Arr. **Timothy Johnson** (ASCAP)

3. FOR THE BEAUTY OF THE EARTH

Dix

Conrad Kocher
Arr. **Dougals Court** (ASCAP)

4. IMMORTAL, INVISIBLE

St. Denio

Traditional Welsh Melody
Arr. **Stephen Bulla** (ASCAP)

Copyright © 2003 by **Curnow Music Press, Inc.**

5. WHEN PEACE LIKE A RIVER

It Is Well With My Soul
Ville Du Havre

Philip P. Bliss

Arr. **James Curnow** (ASCAP)

Track: 7 17

6. COME, YE THANKFUL PEOPLE, COME

St. George's, Windsor

George J. Elvey
Arr. **Paul Curnow** (ASCAP)

Track: 8 18

7. O WORSHIP THE KING
Lyons

Johann Michael Haydn
Arr. **Timothy Johnson** (ASCAP)

8. TO GOD BE THE GLORY

William H. Doane
Arr. **Douglas Court** (ASCAP)

9. CROWN HIM!
Diademata

George J. Elvey
Arr. **Paul Curnow** (ASCAP)

Brilliantly (♩ = 108 - 112)

36

10. FAIREST LORD JESUS
Crusader's Hymn

Traditional
Arr. **Stephen Bulla** (ASCAP)

Tranquil and flowing (♩ = 72)

Copyright © 2003 by **Curnow Music Press, Inc.**